TRAINING GROUND

From Anointing to Appointing

TAYLOR PHILLIPS

UNITED HOUSE

ISBN: 978-1-952-84003-6

UNITED HOUSE Publishing
Waterford, Michigan
info@unitedhousepublishing.com
www.unitedhousepublishing.com

Cover and interior design:
Matt Russell, Marketing Image, mrussell@marketing-image.com

Printed in the United States of America
2020—First Edition

SPECIAL SALES
Most UNITED HOUSE books are available at special quantity discounts when purchased in bulk by corporations, organizations, and special-interest groups. For information, please e-mail orders@unitedhousepublishing.com

While I could write another book full of dedications, there are two people I want to specifically dedicate this book to: my husband, who is my rock, and my best friend, my encourager, challenger, and supporter. This is our story; our journey, and I wouldn't trade it for the world.

To Kristi Miller: Thank you for calling this book out of me.

CONTENTS

INTRODUCTION

Imagine with me for a minute: You are standing in front of the CFO, CEO, and board of directors at the most prestigious company you can think of, interviewing for a top-level management position. You see them smile with satisfaction as they glance through your impressive resume.

"You are hired!" they exclaim.

Breathing a sigh of relief, you excitedly thank them. They tell you Monday is your start date and to report to HR to receive a key to your office.

Monday arrives, and you are dressed to the nines. Confidence radiates from you.

Stepping off the elevator at HR, you let them know you're the new manager. Without making eye contact with you, they hand you a pair of overalls, gloves, and a hard hat. Confused, you repeat that you're the new manager, and you're there to get keys and directions to your new office. In a monotone voice, they tell you your office will be on the ground floor working at the lowest level of employment in the company.

Incredulous, you storm up to the CEO's office and demand to know why you're being placed at the lowest position.

"Your talent and skills for a management level position are impeccable," he tells you. "However, you don't know how this company runs, nor every area of employment. In order for you to effectively manage from the top position, we are requiring you to learn the foundation of the company by starting at the ground level and working your way up to the position we've hired you for."

Though the scenario is fictional, the concept is not. Many of us have been in this position in one way or another. In the Christian world, we hear a lot about calling and being anointed by God for a specific position to carry His gospel forth and make His name known. However, just like we often must start out at ground level in a new job, we often have to start at ground level in our calling and work our way up.

In a social media-saturated world where success looks as simple as writing a viral post, sharing a funny video, or creating a course, it's easy to get caught up in the excitement of 'overnight success.' However, walking in our calling looks similar to the story I shared about the new manager position. You're hired (anointed) for a position, but you're thrust into a lower-level position to build a foundation, and often, the lowest level of employment is where you're the most unseen.

Being called by God isn't about being seen and adored by people. It's about living a life of authenticity and purity, so, when people see us living the way we do, they're drawn to the King of Kings and the Lord of Lords who lives within us. It's not about our gifts and talents, how much money we can make, or how successful we are; it's about making Christ known. The Christian journey isn't a sprint, but one of endurance. In order to be able to endure long, God takes us through a process where He removes our old fleshly foundation and replaces it with one built on His word and His character.

Unfortunately, some decide they don't want to go through the process and quit right there, or they force their way into positions and find themselves discouraged and falling away. Those who allow God to strip away everything that does not glorify Him, those that lean on Him, and trust in His strength and provision are the ones that stand, even when it gets hard.

The process isn't about gaining visibility to the world, but it's about gaining a closer relationship with Him. It's a purity of heart He desires for us to have.

That's what this book is about. Just as the CEO in the story recognized the potential, God knows your potential. However, in order for us to effectively operate, we must go through a training process to restructure our foundation.

Each of these chapters addresses heart issues that manifest in different ways. I encourage you to read this book with an open heart and an open mind and allow God to move and restructure your heart as He so desires.

So receive my correction no matter how hard it is to swallow, for wisdom will snap you back into place—her words will be invigorating life to you. (Proverbs 4:13, TPT)

CHAPTER 1

The Heart that Runs Ahead

There is a myriad of emotions when we figure out what God has called us to do. We might experience timidity or hesitancy because we're unsure, we might be so excited we want to do it immediately because we have a purpose, or we know it's what we're supposed to do but we know it isn't quite time.

I used to fall under the "I'm so excited and I want to do it NOW!" category. I probably could have run for a government office in "making things happen." When God called me to do something, I wanted to make it happen yesterday. I didn't feel the need to grow into anything, to learn more, or to seek the Lord about it. After all, He called me to it, obviously I'm equipped in every area already, right?

Not quite.

One thing we must realize is God has called us, yes, but there is a process of growth that takes place as we walk toward the final destination and fulfill what God has called us to. This process removes our fleshly nature, a nature that doesn't always glorify God, and teaches us to be more like Him.

We know God has called us to something magnificent, beyond our wildest imagination. There is an attitude of excitement when we finally realize what it is we were made to do. Nothing is going to stop us from doing it, least of all people. We start finding the right connections, we say the right things, we work a little, and then we start doing what we *know* God has called us to do, even if moving quickly isn't what God has *asked* us to do.

We live in an "instant gratification" world. Everything is at our disposal within minutes. We are taught to move quickly, get our foot in the door before anyone else, and make stuff happen. But then we get discouraged because we don't have much support from people. People aren't showing up, they're not buying our product, they're not watching our videos, they're not listening to us. We start to wonder, "Was this really the right move?" and we grow tired of our "doing."

I quickly learned that I grew the most tired when I was making things happen myself instead of letting God bring them about in His timing. I quickly learned when I focused on seeking His face, He revealed a better way, a better plan, and better positions. I can tell you when you make His face your sole focus, He will put you in places to make His name great, regardless if those positions look great to us or not.

You have probably been on a treadmill at some point in your life and have tried to go as fast as you could. Have you ever gotten off the treadmill, turned it up to a high speed, and then tried to jump back on it and keep the pace?

I did as a kid, and I have a scar to show for it. My friends and

I thought it would be fun to turn the treadmill up to the highest setting and take turns trying to keep up. I was volun-told to go first, so I psyched myself up and got a running start, jumped on the treadmill, and kept up with it for a few seconds. The next thing I knew, I lost my footing, flew off the treadmill, and found myself caught between the exercise machine and the wall. My elbow and knee were scraped up from the accident.

Why did I fall off? It wasn't only because I wasn't fast enough; it was because I wasn't built to remain at that speed. When you are on a treadmill, you start at a walk, and then you begin to accelerate your speed. It's silly to start out at full speed because you know the chances of injury are higher.

It is so easy to continue increasing the pace on a treadmill. There are times in interval training I think, *I am going so slow*! So, I hit the acceleration button, only to realize I would have to continue running at that speed (or faster) for longer than I thought. What I fail to remember is that the slower speed was meant for my recovery so I could better build my endurance for the faster intervals.

It is easy to adopt the "increase the speed" mindset with something God has asked you to do. In our excitement of the first step we receive from God, we plan out the next twenty steps.

He said to start writing! I should find a publishing company. Increasing the speed by 1.2.

I need to tell everyone God told me I've been called to lead a Bible study! Increasing the speed by 2.0.

He told me I would be the CEO! I need to start getting involved in everything right now, so I know how it's run. Increasing the speed by 2.5.

Working toward goals, planning, and dreaming are not bad. I have dreams, goals, and visions. They are necessary. God says in Proverbs 29:18 people perish for lack of vision. So, I'm not saying working towards goals is bad, nor is effort to achieve those goals wrong. We need to be reminded that when God calls us, He also equips us for that calling. It's not something we're immediately ready to do. Instead of trusting the process He is taking us through, we wear ourselves out by trying to take matters into our own hands. If we sit back and understand the slower speed is aiding in our endurance, we would have fewer injuries and more personal records. We are not meant to go at breakneck speed and remain at that high speed.

You can move when you want, or you can move when God says move. There's a difference between a Spirit-timed move and a flesh-timed move. This tension between timing is what was taking place in the story of Ishmael and Isaac.

If you're not familiar with the Bible, in the book of Genesis, chapters 15-17, there is a man by the name of Abram. God tells Abram He is going to make him the father of many nations, and God changes Abram's name to Abraham, and his wife's name from Sarai to Sarah. This promise took a long time to manifest; twenty-five years to be exact. During this time, Sarah grew impatient and decided to tell her husband to sleep with her slave, named Hagar, to have an heir. Ishmael was born of Hagar, though Ishmael was not the promise God had in mind.

To recap the story, God appears to Abram in a vision and reminds him He is his reward. Abram immediately asks God about the situation of the child. In his humanness, the only thing he can see is one of his slaves being the heir that was part of God's promise. It is here God expounds on what He told Abram a few chapters before. He tells Abram it would be a son that would come from his own body who would be the heir, not his slave, Eliezer. God continues to tell Abram what will happen to his descendants, and He ends by entering a covenant with Abram, signifying God would be true to His word. Shortly after this, Abram's wife, Sarai, approaches him about sleeping with her maidservant, Hagar. Abram willingly agreed to do so. After Abram sleeps with the maidservant, God reminds him of the promise of a son from *his own body* by changing Abram and Sarai's names to Abraham and Sarah.

Now, before you pass judgment on Abraham, I want to submit to you we do the exact same thing—we may not sleep with a maidservant, but we compromise. We take the word God has given us and we create the rest of the narrative based on how we see it taking place.

Remember, his wife was barren, meaning she could not have children. So, her solution fit what God said to Abram earlier. It wasn't like he was adopting a child, no, the child would *be a son from his own body.* He did not even take into consideration his wife would have a child because God did not say that to him. So, Abram filled in the blanks and said, "Okay, I'll do it."

We do the same. We don't get the full word from God, so we fill in the blanks and take the situation into our own hands, when, what we should do is go *back* to God and ask for more insight. The temptation is to "push" the promise based on a partial word from God because we don't want to wait any longer and because, "God said it yesterday, so it must be happening *today.*"

We've all had an Abraham and Sarah moment where our desires got in the way of obedience and where the excitement of the next thing led us to create promises of the flesh. Anything that we have been called to do, we must prepare for, so we must go through a stripping. Abraham had been through a stripping process. He was told to leave a land he was familiar with and go to a land God would show him. Throughout Abraham's life, God stripped him of everything that would cause him to seek outside resources to bring to pass the promise God had spoken.

Not only do we have to go through a stripping, but we must go through a training of sorts. We must learn how to do what God has called us to do. It is like being hired to work for a company. They don't tell us what our job description will be or opportunities for promotion and then immediately put us in that position. We must go through training and learn how to do the job. Just because God has called us to a place does not mean there won't be a time of growth before the promotion.

I have a few Ishmaels in my life. One is a devotional book. Actually, several of my "almost" Ishmaels have dealt with books. I have known authoring books is something God has gifted me to do, and so when the opportunity presented itself in the past, I jumped too early.

Several years ago, I received a phone call from a self-publishing company. They wanted to help me publish a book, and they wanted to start the process of getting a manuscript together. I was so excited. It was finally my opportunity to step into what God was calling me to do! I knew better than to get ahead of God, so I sought Him before I committed. I sensed it wasn't time yet, and I wasn't ready to write on the topic they had inquired about, so I declined the offer.

I continued being faithful in writing and studying and growing closer to God. It was about a year later when I sensed in my spirit it was time to start the process of writing a devotional. I had many people asking me how I learned so much from Scripture, what devotional I was working on, and if I could teach them how to study the Bible, so that's what I wrote about.

However, there was a small issue. God told me to *begin* the process and be faithful in the writing. What I translated that into was I needed to hurry through it and get it published. After all, *so many* were waiting for it to come out. I wrote it in a month, self-published it so I wouldn't have to go through the process of finding a publishing company, and I waited on the royalties to flow in and lives to be changed. Instead, I got fewer royalties than I had imagined, more critiques than I wanted, and I became really self-conscious of the material I had released. Not that it wasn't biblically based, it just wasn't… *it*. So, I went back to God.

"God, I thought you said it was time to start writing!"

"I did," I heard in my spirit, "I didn't say it was time to crank out a devotional and publish it."

It was then I realized I had gone ahead of God and created the rest of the promise based on what I believed God would have me to do. You would think that would cause me to learn my lesson, and it did—but only in the area of publishing books. I have many other instances where I took a promise from God, and I made it happen in my time.

It isn't that Ishmaels, or our own plans, are inherently bad; it's that they are birthed from our flesh. Ishmaels are the reminder that we moved ahead of God, and as a result, we didn't experience the full blessing He had intended for us to walk in.

Nations were born from both Ishmael *and* Isaac, but it was from Isaac that Israel was birthed, and it was through Isaac's lineage that Jesus was born. We may think we have our own best interest in mind and think the way we would do something is the best way, however, our lives are not meant to only impact those in our immediate sphere of influence. Our impact will also create a future built upon the obedience of our now.

In a world wrapped up in purpose, it is easy to get caught up in wondering who you are and what it is you were created to do, especially if it isn't massive or obviously impactful. It's easy to get caught up in wondering if what you are doing is meaningful and effective because of what is seen on social media. Your calling, ministry, or purpose does not have to be massive and well-known to be effective.

Our very first purpose is intimacy with Him. God is a relational God. He doesn't call you to Him through the Holy Spirit to give you instructions and send you on your way. He calls you to Him to be in relationship with Him, to hear His heart for you, and to walk in union with Him. Our purpose, our calling, or what we do, is simply an overflow of our time spent with Him.

Sometimes, we get wrapped up in performance, thinking if we *do*, He will love us and accept us. He's already accepted us and chosen us as His beloved. He proved that when Jesus died on the cross for our sins. We don't walk out what He's called us to in order to prove our love to Him, we walk it out *because* we are loved by Him, and His love compels us to action to display His glory and goodness in our lives.

When our focus is Him, and we spend time with Him in worship and prayer, the Holy Spirit begins to remove the veil that once separated us. We see and experience His character; we come to know His voice, and we respond to Him. When our sole focus is Him and being in a relationship with Him, Ishmaels are harder to come by and Isaacs are birthed naturally. Everything we do, from raising children to running businesses will be impactful because He is our main focus.

CHAPTER 2

The Heart that Doubts God's Timing

When I was in grade school, my friends and I loved Double Dutch. For those of you who are unfamiliar, it's a game where you have two jump ropes going at the same time, in the same space, in opposite directions. The goal is to run and jump in without messing up the motion of the jump ropes.

It is all about timing in the game of Double Dutch. The ropes must be staggered, otherwise, you risk the chance of jumping over one but catching the other. Once you time your jump right, you can speed up as you get your footing and mindset.

As I've grown in my ability to wait on God's "go," I've learned the importance of timing. Like with the example of the treadmill from the previous chapter, you must wait for the right time to make the next move. God hasn't called us to fall on our faces. He isn't asking us to go at a speed that we cannot handle. He isn't a God who pushes us to a pace prone to injury.

This does not mean in waiting you won't make forward progress. In fact, waiting on God is when you progress the most because you are better prepared for when God says "go."

Personally, I know God has called me to write and speak. It was a clear word I knew beyond the shadow of a doubt at twenty years old. I was at a Christian conference when I felt the call of God. What I didn't know is how I would get there.

Since I've received that call, it's been a process of growing into it. It has been trial and error of moving correctly but mostly moving too fast. It truly has been a game of Double Dutch.

I like knowing where I'm going and when it's taking place. When I travel, I want to know the approximate time we are leaving and when we might arrive. If we are going to see family, they'll get several texts along the way of arrival time updates. If we have a hotel booked, and we're going to be late, I will call and let them know.

When I am driving in an unfamiliar town, I want to know several directions at the same time: where I am to make the first turn and what is coming after that.

This has been one area where I struggle because I do not like delay of any kind. My husband can attest to this. When preparing to leave on any trip, I am pacing, uptight, a little snappy, and ready to go. I have no idea why; it's not like it's possible to wake up one moment and be on the road instantaneously, but if I had my way, that's exactly what we would do.

Over the last eight years, I've had to trust God's timing in my life and work hard not to force things to happen in my timing. In the last chapter, we talked about Ishmael and Isaac, and in this chapter, I want to expound on walking in the timing of God.

Pastor Craig Groeschel of Life Church said, "If it's not in God's timing, you can't force it. If it is in God's timing, you can't stop it."[1]   While this sounds good and is encouraging and is true in many situations, I believe it's not something that can be blanketed across every situation. For example, Abraham and Sarah could tell you that you can *attempt to force* the timing of God.

In Genesis 17, God told Abraham He would give him a son through his wife, Sarah. After Abraham laughed, he said this:

> *And Abraham said to God, 'Oh that Ishmael might live before you!' God said, 'No, but Sarah your wife shall bear you a son, and you shall call his name Isaac. I will establish my covenant with him as an everlasting covenant for his offspring after him.'* (Genesis 17:18-19, ESV)

God said "no" when Abraham asked that Ishmael might live before him. For the last thirteen years, Ishmael had been Abraham's only son, therefore, the heir of whatever Abraham had. However, God's plan was not meant to be carried out through Ishmael, which is why he said "no." That didn't mean Ishmael would be abandoned because God told Abraham he would bless Ishmael too, but, the promise God intended from the beginning wasn't to happen through Ishmael.

It's like trying to pick an unripe apple while at the same time saying it won't come off until it's time. If you pick it, it'll still come off the tree. What's different is the taste and the aftermath. While you might not be able to force the timing of God, you *can* create a cheap substitute of the promise coming to pass.

There are times that, no matter how much you pray, something doesn't happen until it's time for it to happen. I believe what it boils down to is obedience. Are you doing what the Lord has prompted you to do, or are you doing something contrary to that word under the guise of 'I can't force God's timing'?

We live in a world where we make things happen. Want a raise? Go to your boss and ask for (or demand) a raise. Don't like how something is being done? Quit and go do something else. We can easily force things to happen and call it the timing of God because it happened. The risk when we do this is we miss out on the fullness, on the sweetness of that complete promise coming to pass, and take up for ourselves something less than what God had intended for us.

Sometimes action is not wrong, and it is a solution. However, not always is it God's solution. What if He's asking you to remain silent and simply work so He can elevate you to a greater position beyond your wildest imagination? What if you're in a hard place so you can minister to those who aren't treating you nicely?

I get it, though. It's all in God's timing has become a cliché saying, and it's frustrating. We want to know what God's timing looks like and when it might happen. However, it's not about *when* it will happen but *how* we will wait and stand *until* we see it happen.

Trusting in God's timing comes down to trusting God's character and believing He will do as He has promised. The issue of whether or not we will see what He has promised come to pass hinges on whether or not we are willing to stand

and obey and see it come to pass.

I cannot think of a better example than in Exodus 4. Here, God meets with Moses, giving Him a word to deliver to the Israelites.

Moses and Aaron brought together all the elders of the Israelites, and Aaron told them everything the Lord had said to Moses. He also performed the signs before the people, and they believed. And when they heard that the Lord was concerned about them and had seen their misery, they bowed down and worshiped. (Exodus 4:29-31, NIV)

Now, we know from reading the rest of Exodus that after so many plagues, God delivers His people from Pharaoh's hand. However, the Israelites did not know this yet. They only knew God said He would deliver them, but they didn't know when. There are many times we receive a message from God, and immediately opposition arises. We might have experienced God in an incredible way at a church service, but we go home, and we are faced with the reality that nothing seems to have changed in our situation.

My husband and I have learned we are to use the prophetic words God has given us in prayer by declaring God's word over our situation. However, even declaring His word over a situation may not change it immediately. Declaring His word will always increase our faith and stamina to stand no matter how hard it gets.

One of the ways that best instills faith in my heart is one that I often forget: recalling God's faithfulness. Often, I am like the Israelites after they've forgotten God's faithfulness in escaping the Egyptians by crossing the Red Sea. I complain and grumble, questioning God's goodness instead of recalling His faithfulness. By His grace, however, I am becoming better at recalling His goodness.

When I sit down and write out all of the ways God has been faithful, whether it's as small as a sunny day when it's been dreary, physically and emotionally, or in a bigger way such as financial provision, I am reminded it's never been God that has changed. Instead, I have focused on my current circumstances more than I have on His faithfulness.

In the journey from anointing to appointing, the temptation will be to finish in our own strength and solve problems in our own understanding, instead of relying on God's sufficient grace to guide us through every step. Frustration about not immediately receiving the next step is real, but we have to trust that if He's not giving us the next step, it's not because we aren't meant for it—it's because it's not time yet. He will reveal the next step when it's time.

I love the scripture in 2 Timothy that tells of a soldier who doesn't get involved in civilian affairs. Here's the thing about the soldier: he doesn't get involved in civilian affairs because he knows it will not only result in distraction from the mission his commanding officer has given but also in disunity and even potential injury.

We have been given a mission: to make Christ known and further the Kingdom of God through discipling. Within that mission is the training to carry out what He has called us to (i.e.

gifts and talents). We cannot get distracted by what is or is not happening, the opinion of those not in the war with us, or step away from our Commanding Officer to run a platoon on our own. A soldier trusts that his commanding officer knows what is going on and can see what he may not see, so he willingly completes the task.

I would encourage you to repent of losing focus on what God is doing and the mission you're on if you've become distracted by civilian affairs. Next, sit down and write a list of all the ways God has been faithful. Nothing is off-limits or silly. Spend time afterward thanking Him for taking care of you. Don't wait until dire circumstances to focus on God's faithfulness, but begin making a daily habit of praise and thanksgiving.

Sometimes, when I am in a low spot, I listen to praise music, and what hits me is a thanksgiving point. For example, if I am struggling to see the bigger picture, I might play Danny Gokey's "Haven't Seen it Yet"[2] and thank Him for His faithfulness in leading and guiding me.

How has God been faithful to you today? How about this week? This month? This year? Don't neglect recalling His goodness and faithfulness. Faith is built and endurance increases with thanksgiving.

CHAPTER 3

The Heart in Need of Preparation

'Preparation time is never wasted time."[3]
Terri Savelle Foy

How are you preparing for the next opportunity? Are you diligently working to improve your gifts and talents, knowing you'll be ready when the next opportunity strikes, or are you sitting idly by, waiting for opportunities to arise believing you'll be prepared because He's called you to it?

You might be wondering how this is different from the first chapter, and whether I'm about to contradict myself. Growth and preparation go hand-in-hand on the journey of walking out what God has intended for us. You can wait on the right time while also preparing to take the next step. Opportunities will come whether we are ready or not.

I like to think of it in terms of a soldier. They are not always on the frontlines battling nor do they go searching for a battle, but they are always preparing for the battle that may or may not happen. When it does happen, the soldier is ready and prepared to win the battle because of the growth and preparation that has taken place beforehand.

I shared about a book opportunity I was given about six years ago. I had been contacted about writing a book on a specific topic. While I *really* wanted to write this book, I knew I had not properly prepared as I had been instructed to, and therefore, I had to pass it up.

After turning it down, I realized I needed to prepare for the next one, whenever that would be.

Much of my preparation has been in private. Notebooks full of unpublished writing, speaking to small groups of people or youth groups, being unknown to many, and waiting on opportunities that have yet to happen. It is easy to get to a place of "what's the point of continuing to prepare?" when you don't see immediate results of your obedience.

I love how Paul tells us to "be prepared in season and out of season" (2 Timothy 4:2, NIV). I know this is referring to sharing the gospel, but I believe it also applies to our daily lives.

It is important to be prepared in season and out of season because you don't know when someone is going to call you in need of what you have to offer. I've had people call me at the last minute and ask me to speak to a group of people within a short period of time. Had I not prepared in private, I would not be prepared to step out publicly.

The greatest NCAA basketball coach of all time, John Wooden once said, "When the opportunity comes, it's too late to prepare."[4]

I love this quote for more reasons than one. It takes me back to my basketball days. Every practice we had was in preparation for an upcoming game. Our coaches had their five starters for every game, but if someone other than those five starters practiced better, you can bet a starter lost their position in the upcoming game. Who played in the game largely depended on who practiced well.

We didn't practice forcing our performance but to hone the talent of playing basketball we already had. It was to go over what we already knew to perform to our greatest potential. If you didn't practice, you didn't play. If you didn't practice, you wouldn't know the plays, and that could cost points during the game.

Preparing for what God has called us to is no different. If you don't practice, you don't play. Practice may look different than what you'd like it to in the season you're in, but do what you know to do, trusting God will make a way in your faithfulness.

Stay prepared to defend your faith and share God's word by studying, reading, and spending time with God.

Stay prepared for the next speaking opportunity by practicing when you converse with others and study the art of speaking.

Stay prepared to write that book by writing every day, even if no one sees it.

Stay prepared by meeting with a mentor to ask questions that will equip you better.

Stay prepared by praying for others, even when it doesn't seem like a grand request.

Like I mentioned before, I figured because God had called me to write and speak, I was ready for it. I didn't know it was only the starting line. I began a race, or more importantly, I had a race to begin training for. I took off running without proper training, and as a result, suffered unnecessary injuries.

During a season of working from home, I began *actually* running with my friend. I was sitting behind a computer or reading several hours out of the day, and my body was not used to that level of inactivity. I joined a friend who ran a few miles over the lunch hour, not realizing through it, I would gain revelation from God about physical training *and* spiritual training.

I ran track in middle school, and I've always enjoyed running between one and five miles. However, outside of basketball and running occasionally when I cheered in college, it was not a priority. So, when I began this lunch-hour running, I had to continually remind myself at twenty-seven years old, I did not have the body I did in middle school or high school.

On my first ever intentional run since college, I agreed to run two miles. As I was stretching, my husband asked me if I thought it was a good idea to run two miles right off the bat. In my head, I thought *Oh yeah, I might have to call you to come pick me up*. But I wasn't about to admit it out loud. So instead I said, "How hard could it be to run two miles?"

My husband was right—agreeing to two miles was a terrible idea. I got home and collapsed on the floor. Every part of my body was screaming in shock over what I forced it to do. My sister had come over to visit, and I couldn't even voice a word. I was so tired. My lungs were on fire, and I was tasting blood. Later, when I Googled it, I learned that strenuous exercise (like what I had put my body through) without proper training is not good on your lungs, and you'll taste blood. I wanted to quit so bad that same day. The pain was miserable, and I didn't feel it was worth it. I'd find another way to be active. But I had agreed to run over the lunch hour. I couldn't quit. I am not someone who quits…especially not first.

I made the decision to at least stick it out for a few weeks and see where I was then. God used those weeks to minister to me about our race as Christians. A week later, I told my running partner of my goal to run one mile straight through. We would set a good pace, and I would try to keep it. It doesn't sound like much, but when you haven't run since college, it's a huge goal.

I was about a half mile in, and my pace was a fast one. Contemplating quitting, I heard, *the Christian race is one of endurance*. I slowed down to chew on this revelation, and after a short period, I realized my lungs weren't on fire, and it was easier to keep going. It became clear to me that if I was going to build up my endurance, I would have to train my body by pacing myself.

Preparation time can seem a lot like treading water: there is no forward momentum, but a lot of strength is being built. Though it seemed like my physical training process had developed quickly with practice, I had to remember that it doesn't always go that quickly.

My husband and I have been in a season of waiting and refining. We were given promises by God several years ago, and we have yet to see any major physical manifestation. We asked God long ago that our lives would be a display of His power and show nothing of us but all of God's goodness. I don't say this in pride but to tell you when you pray prayers like that, you have to be prepared to go through a stripping process to reach that point. We have been in situations where there seemed to be no way out; where all we could do was blindly trust and obey Him. We have been stripped of every single Plan B and crutch, and all we've been left with is each other and God. We hold on to the promise this time is preparing us for something greater.

We have had to train ourselves to hear God's "yes" in this season, because for so many years, it had been "no" or "wait." We have endured ridicule, shame, mocking, condemnation, cursing, and slander. We've battled fear, anxiety, anger, confusion, hopelessness, doubt, and shame. We have learned it's not about us or what we receive, but it's about fully surrendering to Him and bringing glory to His name.

Oftentimes, after receiving a prophetic word, the opposite of that word happens. You don't step immediately into the promise, but you survive the opposite to create endurance and root His promise further in your heart. It's that much sweeter when it comes to pass. It is necessary and probably one of the hardest journeys. In the middle, between the promise received and the promise manifested is where you learn the motive of your heart. How to honor when it's difficult, how to stand on God's word to see it come to pass in your life, how to root yourself in Him, and how to not be defined by what people say, but what God says.

If you want to be anointed for a position, you are going to have to go through a time of training that seems impossible. When you sign up for the military, you don't go to war. You have to understand the basics and learn about how the branch of military operates. Though there are different positions within the military, everyone goes through basic training. If one chooses to go on and further their military career, there is training that has to be endured in order to excel.

God is the same. He is not going to give you something void of preparation. We are always preparing for the next thing God has for us. We don't know what is next, but every training day is preparing us for each opportunity we will be given.

I love what Jesus says about proper training:

The one who manages the little he has been given with faithfulness and integrity will be promoted and trusted with greater responsibilities. But those who cheat with the little they have been given will not be considered trustworthy to receive more. (Luke 16:10, TPT)

We have to start managing small things before we are trusted with the big things. You don't give a new medical student a brain surgeon's job until he has trained.

Even if you have a glimpse of what you are called to do, there *is* a stripping process we *all* must endure to remove the flesh and get down to an authentic relationship with God. He isn't concerned about our status but the status of our heart. God's desire is for us to experience freedom and to experience all He has for us, but we have a lot of junk from life that needs to come out before we can experience the fullness of it.

There are a lot of people who want to be in a position of influence but haven't counted the cost or are unwilling to count the cost of that position. It would seem with filtered photos on social media that influence comes easy with the right picture or caption. We see phrases like "make this go viral," or "you've gone viral." Overnight success seems achievable with the movement of your fingers on the keyboard or recording a video.

What we often forget, or don't realize, is there is no such thing as an overnight success. Not only that, but success is different for everyone. We've created a world where you're only successful if you're visible and do something with an important title. We don't see the behind the scenes of someone's life. We don't know how they conduct themselves or the sacrifices they have or haven't made to get to where they are. We only see the final, filtered result.

I think we are so hungry to be used by God in such a way that nothing is the same after He uses us. Here's the thing: whether or not we want to be used by God on a stage, or we want to serve Him in unseen ways, we aren't cheap china. Our worth is far greater than cheap plastic used once and thrown away. Cheap plastic cannot withstand the pressure put on it.

I don't care if you speak to 30,000 people, sing at a sold-out concert, preach to a congregation of 200, volunteer, or scrub toilets: we all experience pressure. If we don't allow God to prepare us and strengthen us, we will crumble under the pressures of life.

God doesn't withhold or keep us from opportunities because He enjoys dangling a carrot in front of us and making us chase what He wants us to do. He tells us to wait and be prepared by Him, so when pressures arise, we look to Him for the strength developed in the secret place. We're prepared so when we succeed in an area, the success doesn't get to our head and change how we treat people. He prepares us to endure so our lives are a display of His glory.

We have too many people settling for a thicker paper plate that resembles fine china so they can hurry up and "be used by God." The pressures of life end up overwhelming them, and they bust in the center where much of the strength is needed.

The Christian walk isn't about how much you can get done by the end of your life or how successful you are or are not. It's not about status or titles. It's about your faithfulness. And faithfulness requires endurance.

When you see people being elevated above you, will you be faithful to continue doing what you've been told to do in that season? Will you try and put yourself in a position to be seen, or will you continue to wait, knowing it's God who promotes? Will you allow heart issues to be dealt with so you can continue progressing?

When you're mistreated, will you remain faithful where He's called you, believing He will bring justice? Or do you quit because of the way you're treated or seek vengeance on your own?

When things aren't moving as fast as you think they should,

and you feel like you've been hidden in the cleft of the rock for so long, what will your response be? Will you try to rush things?

When you receive a prophetic word, what will you do with it? Will you seek His face for more, or will you take what you have and make the rest of it up? We must be willing to go through a process so the image inside of us is the image of God, not the image of man.

Preparation isn't for positions of influence, but it's for removing what would cause separation from God or be a stumbling block for others. If we come to a place where everything were to pass away, every opportunity to be seen or make a large impact, and we still choose Him, our hearts are right, and we're ready for the next thing God has for us.

Sometimes, we learn lessons the hard way, and that's okay. We are sinners, and often, it takes a few tries for us to understand that God's way is best. If that's you, and you feel like you've messed it up, don't think you're past help. You can start wherever you are at and allow Him to transform your heart and mind.

I want to speak to those who feel called to the stage for a moment. There is nothing wrong with that desire, and I'm not writing to not desire that position. Those are God-given desires. But, here's the thing: we have enough people who desire the platform without the proper preparation to withstand the trials in getting there. If our motive is to be seen by people and not to bring God glory, we shouldn't be doing something in Jesus' name. There is pressure to prove and to perform, and we can get caught up in the numbers we speak to, basing success off of those numbers. There's a temptation to think you've arrived and neglect your duties elsewhere. But, it's not about you. When you step on stage, you are you. When you step off the stage, you are you. You are not some special, anointed person who is exempt from continuing to walk in a manner worthy of the calling. No. If anything, you are called to a higher standard, to walk it out in humility *because* you are in front of people. If you step up on stage and preach to an audience they need to walk a certain way, but you aren't doing it yourself, you're a hypocrite. If you step on stage and talk about being a good servant within your church, but you see yourself as more valuable because you're preaching to the masses and don't continue to humbly serve, you're a hypocrite.

We have enough hypocrites in this life, making a relationship with Jesus repulsive to many. He isn't calling us to hypocrisy but *intimacy with Him*, creating an authenticity that draws people to *Him*. You cannot sustain a life of visible humility if you are not first humbled and surrendered before God, allowing Him to correct you. We are to be carriers of His glory, drawing others into a personal relationship that transforms them and the world around them. But, if we live like the world, we're only going to recreate the world. There won't be any bringing heaven to earth when we're caught up in what *we* do and how successful *we* are.

We have been called to make Christ known. If we are too busy promoting our own gospel and promoting ourselves, the gospel of Jesus Christ isn't being preached, and instead of leading others to Christ, we're leading others to us. That's a dangerous place to be, my friend, because then people start leaving the truth of God's word for fables. When we begin to follow man-made theology, we risk leaving the gospel of Jesus Christ. It is dangerous to take God's glory for yourself. It is His glory in you. Rejoice in what He's doing through you, but don't think for a moment it's all you.

How is God asking you to prepare? Please understand I'm not referring to forcing the promise. We can prepare for what we've prayed for without forcing it. Is there somewhere He has called you to sacrifice? Is there an area you can grow your knowledge in? Is there a gift or a talent you can practice?

Whatever you feel He is asking you to do, even if it doesn't make sense, do it. You don't know the upcoming opportunities He may have you be part of because you've been faithful to stay ready.

CHAPTER 4

The Heart in Need of Freedom

My car sat in my driveway for a few weeks because it would not accelerate. No matter how much gas you gave it, it would not go forward. You could go slow and get it somewhere, but that was the extent of my traveling.

When we got it to a mechanic, he informed us it was my catalytic converter. Now, I'm no mechanic or car guru, so I had to look it up. The catalytic converter deals with the exhaust. In layman's terms, the catalytic converter is an area in which a controlled combustion can take place to make the vehicle's engine run smoothly. If one is clogged, it results in lessened acceleration and power, which is what I was experiencing.

Long story short, the catalytic converter on the back of my vehicle was clogged up and not allowing the exhaust to be emitted. It was cleaned out and taken care of, and my car has run like a charm ever since. It probably runs better than before.

There are things in life that cause our "catalytic converters" to be clogged. Life experiences marked by disappointment, excitement, change, words, and other incidents lead to clogs that keep our engines from running effectively. Whether we are running with our own two feet or driving a car, the author of Hebrews tells us we are in a race, and in order to run the race effectively, we must throw off everything that hinders us.

Therefore, since we are surrounded by such a huge crowd of witnesses to the life of faith, let us strip off every weight that slows us down, especially the sin that so easily trips us up. And let us run with endurance the race God has set before us.
(Hebrews 12:1, NLT)

The Greek word for "lay aside" (or strip off), is the word **apotithémi**, which means "to lay off or aside, renounce, stow or put away."[5]

You've probably seen serious runners wearing thin clothing and lightweight running shoes. If you're a runner, you've probably worn the least amount of clothing possible. Why is that? Because if they have more than what is needed, it slows them down and works against their progress. You don't want to add anything that may potentially distract you (as if the screaming of your lungs and legs isn't enough). I've even heard of male runners shaving their legs and wearing those toe shoes, so their level of endurance is at maximum capacity.

That's what the author of Hebrews is saying: strip off what's going to hinder you or what is already hindering you running the race you're in. This scripture also indicates something else to me: there is a difference between what hinders you and sin. You may not necessarily be bogged down by sin, but something may be hindering your ability to run.

Just like my car, you don't need more power. You need to remove the excess preventing your acceleration. There are things that happen to us, whether in our formative years or adulthood, that create a standard by which we think and act. We can become slaves to our habits, mental conversations, coping mechanisms, and addictions and see it as "who we are." However, "who we are" isn't always who God has called us to be.

Bondage and hindrances keep us from experiencing the fullness of what God has to offer us. Oftentimes, we don't know we are in bondage until we taste freedom. Freedom in Christ isn't like freedom offered by the world. Freedom offered by the world creates a greater bondage and makes us search for more of what doesn't heal us. The world tells us to cope with our hurts and disappointments by numbing the pain. Freedom in Christ is acknowledging those hurts and disappointments and taking them to the feet of the Father, allowing Him to remove the hurts. In doing this, our desire for more of God grows.

Growing up, I struggled with self-image. Different debilitating circumstances, hurtful comments, and binding belief systems had me chained to insecurity. I didn't believe I had worth. I may not have portrayed it, but inside all I believed was I wasn't worth two cents. I was negative and couldn't take a compliment because I didn't believe people were being genuine. I had known Christ from a young age but still walked in bondage. It wasn't until I met my husband that I began to see the other side of the coin.

Freedom is as much about trusting God as it is breaking free from bondage. The truth may be you're struggling with a negative mindset or addiction, but it's trusting that because Christ set you free, you're free. It's not an excuse to continue sinning but an opportunity to do the opposite of what you've been stuck in *because* Christ made a way.

For me, I didn't realize fear dictated the majority of my decisions until I tasted peace that surpassed everything I ever knew. I didn't realize I had trouble trusting God fully because I was afraid of betrayal, until He brought me into an intimate knowledge of who He is while I was at a conference. I didn't realize negative words formed and defined my actions until I began hearing what God said about me. It wasn't until I experienced freedom I realized how bound I was by hurts, disappointments, and a mental ideology of myself.

Even though I saw the other side of the coin concerning self-image, I still had a choice to make. When those thoughts of worthlessness popped into my mind, I had to decide: would I agree with them or would I believe what God said about me? There were times I didn't *feel* worthy or free, but I had also been stuck in that mindset for a long time. I had to rewire my brain to believe what God said about me by trading the truth of what I believed about myself with the truth of God's word.

Galatians 5:1 tells us, "So Christ has truly set us free" (NLT). We can live free of insecurity, shame, guilt, addiction, comparison, and the like. We don't *have* to live in those. It isn't easy, but we have the opportunity to choose something different than our struggles. It is important we renew our minds in the word of God so we can walk according to His word. Many are still in bondage as Christians because they have not renewed their minds in God's word. We are told in Psalm 119:45 how His

Word provides freedom.

It's like when you recognize you have been eating too much ice cream and packed on the pounds. To change the habit, you should stop eating ice cream and replace it with exercise or a healthier food. Freedom from sin and bondage is the same. You recognize what has been wrong in your life, stop by repenting, and begin to replace the previous action with what glorifies God.

Freedom is important to walk in because if you're not walking free, you're walking as a captive to whatever is binding you. It sounds obvious, but until we experience something different, or until a new truth is presented to us, we don't know we're slaves to fear, addiction, anger, insecurity, or worry. Until we're aware of what enslaves us, we'll make decisions based on our slavery. When we realize we have been set free by the blood of Jesus Christ, we can make decisions based on the freedom God has given us.

Freedom doesn't come without a fight. It doesn't magically come when we decide we want to be free. It's an all-out war for our freedom, but we can rest in the knowledge that Christ has already won the final war. We may have to fight daily to keep our freedom mindset, but in Christ, we *are* already free. With the help of the Holy Spirit, we grab onto our freedom like a bulldog, and when we are tired, we know Jesus has it, whether we feel it or not. Sometimes, we have to separate from what we know and what might be comfortable to experience the freedom God has for us.

In Genesis 13:5-13, we read about Abraham and Lot having to

separate because of a quarrel among their shepherds. Abraham told Lot to choose where he wanted to go, and wherever he chose, Abraham would go the opposite direction.

Lot looked around and saw that the whole plain of the Jordan toward Zoar was well watered, like the garden of the Lord, like the land of Egypt. (This was before the Lord destroyed Sodom and Gomorrah.) So Lot chose for himself the whole plain of the Jordan and set out toward the east. The two men parted company: Abram lived in the land of Canaan, while Lot lived among the cities of the plain and pitched his tents near Sodom. Now the people of Sodom were wicked and were sinning greatly against the Lord.
(Genesis 13:10-13, NIV)

Lot pitched his tent toward Sodom, a place where the people were wicked and sinning against God. It wasn't long before Lot came to live *in* Sodom.

If we think of our minds as our tent, it matters where we set it up at. What we pitch our tent near, it won't be long before we're in. Whatever we allow our minds to be influenced by, we'll end up part of. So, when we influence our minds with God's word and the things of God, our minds will be renewed, and we will walk holy and blameless lives. However, if we continue to pitch our tents toward our old ways, we will find ourselves still battling the same old things.

I would encourage you, if you are still struggling with returning to your old way of living, to examine where you have allowed your mind to pitch a tent. Everything preaches a message to our hearts and minds; from the friends we have to the movies we watch. Any message that is continually preached will become truth to our minds.

While freedom is a battle, it's a battle worth fighting. It's not an overnight victory. You will face temptation to revisit your old way of living because it felt good and satisfied your flesh. Freedom is different for every area of bondage, but there's one major emotion over them all: peace. The peace you experience is like your favorite comfort food on a hard day. It's a level of rootedness that anchors your soul in knowing beyond a shadow of doubt you are loved, you are free, and you are His. The battle is already won.

CHAPTER 5

The Heart Afraid of Surrender

I suspect one of the most internalized questions for Christians is probably, "How do I surrender to God?"

If you grew up like me, you learned surrender was something you prayed when you accepted Jesus Christ as Savior. Not only that, but there are songs we sing on Sunday's mentioning the word "surrender," but do any of us know what it means?

I think because of our digital world, we are not sure how to surrender, as we have not seen an *image* of it, one that shows us a step-by-step process of the correct way to surrender. I have found myself in the place of wondering if I'm doing it right because I haven't seen an example I believed to be true.

I often forget there *is* an image of surrender right in front of me. He surrendered His life to His Father, endured the cross for us, and is now seated at the right hand of the Father. His name is Jesus.

On the night of His crucifixion, Jesus pleaded with God to take the cup of suffering from Him three times. Ending His prayer those three times were the words, "Yet not as I will, but as You will" (Matthew 26:39b, NIV).

That simple prayer was a prayer of surrender to His Father.

The definition of surrender is "to give oneself up into the power of another; to yield to the power, control, or possession of another upon compulsion or demand."[6]

As humans our natural tendency is to seek control and be in charge. We want to plan our days, our lives, and our responses to events so we always know what is going on. If we don't have a career path marked out before us, we're subject to being tossed to and fro. Growing up, we are taught to decide what *we* want and *how* we are going to get what we want.

Think about it: when you were in school, were you asked what career you wanted to have when you were older? When you had an idea, the next question that usually followed was how are you going to achieve the goal? Would you go to school or immediately get a job in the career field where you could gain experience?

Though having an idea of what you want to achieve in life is good, I believe the desire can deviate into dangerous territory if it causes a hesitation to surrender to God and what He wants to do in your life.

When we accept Christ as our Lord and Savior, we don't seem to think much about what surrender looks like. In the world today, it has been insinuated that a relationship with Christ is as simple as going to church every Sunday and doing good deeds, riding on the coattails of other Christians until we get to heaven. But God has not meant for us to barely get by in this life. He has called us to a greater way of living that will cause us to experience Him in powerful ways.

We must remember His original design for mankind was communion; He would commune and dwell with us. That's how it was designed in the Garden of Eden. But because sin came through Adam and Eve, we experienced separation from God, breaking the communication lines to intimacy. However, Jesus redeemed it all on the cross by dying for our sins and restoring intimacy and communication with God the Father.

I have seen people accept Christ as their Savior because they believe God can serve them and make them great and put them at the top of wherever they want to be. And while God does bless us in ways like that, His original design for us is intimacy with Him. And intimacy requires surrender. It is not in our fleshly nature to yield to something we can't see; it's not in our fleshly nature to surrender our lives to God. I used to think when I surrendered my life to God, I would be sent overseas as a missionary to Africa. I was hesitant to surrender my life to Him because I had an image of what I thought my life should look like, and I believed if I gave my life over to Him, He would ask me to do something I wouldn't like.

I quickly learned surrendering to God doesn't mean He's going to make me do something I don't want to do. Surrendering to God, for me, has looked like laying my life down before Him, trusting Him, and knowing He has a better plan for my life. It was learning more about Him and His character so I could see He wasn't out to take my ideas and change them for my misery. He would take my dreams and my ambitions, line them up according to His Word, and remove my flesh from the equation so He would be the one to get the glory.

I used to believe once I became a Christian, He would change my dreams and ambitions. I have since learned those dreams and ambitions are things He has placed deep within me that need to be washed in His Word and transformed by the Holy Spirit, so I'm not the one getting the glory but Him. What we do is not about us or our success, but it's about living in such a way that causes others to see a life following God is far better than wandering aimlessly on this earth. It is walking in such a way that pulls people from the flames of hell and into the gates of heaven.

One of my favorite stories is the story of Abraham and Isaac on the mountain. Abraham was 100 years old when the long-awaited promise of a son came to pass. Then, God instructed Abraham to go to the land of Moriah and sacrifice Isaac as a burnt offering.

Prior to this instruction, Abraham had been through a stripping process. All the stripping had brought Abraham to this moment. He knew what God had spoken, and He promised him he would be the father of many nations. The promise would come through Isaac, a son born of Abraham and Sarah. He had tried once before with Sarah's maidservant, Hagar, and was told Ishmael was not who the promise of the everlasting covenant would come through. With the knowledge and the stripping Abraham had gone through, would he surrender his one and only son, the son through whom the promised everlasting covenant would come?

Abraham and Isaac set off for the land of Moriah. On the third day, Abraham saw the mountain where he and Isaac would go. He told his servants, "Stay here with the donkey; I and the boy will go over there and worship and come again to you" (Genesis 22:5, ESV).

Abraham was so confident in the promise and the word of God, he told his servants he *and the boy* would be back. He tied the wood and laid it on Isaac and took the fire and knife and walked to the mountain. Isaac wondered what was going on, asking where the lamb was for the offering. Abraham's response? God will provide the lamb.

When they came to the place of which God had told him, Abraham built the altar there and laid the wood in order and bound Isaac his son and laid him on the altar, on top of the wood. Then Abraham reached out his hand and took the knife to slaughter his son. But an angel of the Lord called to him from heaven and said, 'Abraham, Abraham!' And he said, 'Here I am.'
He said, 'Do not lay your hand on the boy or do anything to him, for now I know that you fear God, seeing you have not withheld your son, your only son, from me.' And Abraham lifted up his eyes and looked, and behold, behind him was a ram, caught in a thicket by his horns. And Abraham went and took the ram and offered it up as a burnt offering instead of his son. (Genesis 22:9-13, ESV)

This passage of scripture convicts me because it begs the question:

How willing am I to sacrifice my promise? Do I desire a deeper relationship with Him or only what He can do for me? Am I willing to give up what I believe He's called me to do because I know obedience to Him far outweighs the happiness I think I'd feel in doing something I enjoy?

Think of what it is you believe He has called you to do. If, today, He asked you to lay it down before Him by sacrificing it, would you do it?

I truly believe we have to come to a point of honesty with ourselves and decide whether or not we want His presence in our life or His performance and provision. If we would choose His hand over His face, do we even deserve the calling He has given us?

Surrender in this area looks different for everyone. One summer, I remember receiving instruction from the Lord to lay down my pen. I wasn't to write in a blog or a book, I was to simply be where He had called me in that moment. At first, I was devastated. I had built up a following, was doing well, and on a roll with blog topics; but I knew I needed to obey.

What followed in those months was a time of growth and turmoil all at the same time. My husband and I experienced one of the most spiritually volatile seasons of our lives to date, spending time in isolation and being hidden in the cleft of the rock because not many could be trusted. The very place we had grown exponentially in our relationship with God, we were told to leave.

Had I disobeyed in laying my pen down, the writing I would have produced would have been in hurt and anger instead of being led by the Spirit of God. It wasn't until about a year later, after healing and recovering from the last season, I felt that it was time to pick up my pen. What I had sacrificed in that season, He had given back to me in greater measure.

There will be a time of testing for our calling. God will test our faithfulness to Him by asking us to surrender everything back to Him. To fully surrender to Him, we must surrender our hurts, pains, fears, failures, sins, and more. Without realizing we are doing it, we can allow bondage and baggage to become our identity to the point we no longer see it as an issue in our lives but a friend.

For me, the fear of being abandoned by God was a friend I did not know I had until I attended my church's women's conference. Knowing the Lord was doing a work in me but not knowing what that work was caused me to wrestle spiritually while there. I remember while in prayer before the last evening service, I kept hearing God speak in my spirit: "I love you, and I'm not leaving you." I thought it was strange because I already knew He wasn't leaving me because His Word said it.

You may have a head knowledge of what His Word says, but it doesn't mean your heart has grasped the revelation of that truth. That's where I was without knowing it. After a powerful message, the altar call was an intimate call to freedom in Christ. There were several flaggers who were surrounding us. It was as if each swipe and snap of the flag snapped our spirits to attention and declared war on every lie the enemy had been speaking to us. One young girl stood in front of me, and as I watched her dance with freedom, the words to the song caught my attention:

"You and I, we've got history. We go way way back. I'm never gonna let you go, I'm never gonna let you go. I never have, I never will."[7]

Something within me crumbled to pieces as I doubled over in tears. I felt hands on my wrists and when I uncovered my eyes, this young girl was wrapping me in her arms and praying for me. Walls began to break, and I thought I would collapse under the weight of their crumbling when another woman came up behind me and placed a Royal Blue flag in my hand, which for me, represented freedom, anointing, and hope.[8] She began to take my hand and twirl the flag, whispering I needed to let it go. Everything in me wanted to throw a temper tantrum. I wanted to throw the flag down, dry up my tears, and leave. What I was feeling was foreign and vulnerable. I remembered telling her, "No."

The disconnect between my spirit and my mind suddenly became clear when I realized He was beckoning me deeper and needed me to surrender. Every prophetic word came to mind as I realized if I wanted to walk in the fullness of intimacy, I needed to obey. I fought my flesh and began to twirl the flag. Before I knew it, I was declaring war over my fight for image, my hurts, and every worry and concern. That evening, I experienced a new level of freedom and surrender.

Had you asked me prior to that evening if I were living and surrendered before God, I would have told you I was. To some degree I was, but there were areas simply covered up instead of surrendered. I grew up in a Christian home and had Christians throughout my family. I accepted Jesus as my Savior at a young age. I don't have a significant story of salvation like some; I simply chose Him. Somewhere along the way, though, I picked up the lie that a deep relationship with Christ was for everyone but me. I believed He was going to figure out who I really was and split, so I lived with this underlying fear God was going to leave me. At the conference, I didn't want to surrender because I was afraid my whole life was a lie and I wasn't truly saved. But that was a lie from the pit of hell.

Surrender is a daily opportunity and choice. Surrender is simply a choice between choosing whether we will believe His Word or our circumstances. It's a choice between our way of living or living in surrender before Him. It's a daily choice between building our own empire or building with God.

Will we choose to bow to the lie saying God doesn't have a purpose for us, or will we surrender to the truth that says He has plans to prosper us and not harm us (Jeremiah 29:11, NIV)? Will we bow to the fear that takes our breath away, or will we rise up and walk in the truth that says He "has not given us a spirit of fear but of power, love, and a sound mind" (2 Timothy 1:7, KJV)? There are things we will endure in this life that may seem like we are alone in a situation. The thing about surrender is, in those moments, we know we aren't alone because we've come to the end of ourselves and we know He is the only One who will satisfy. Despite appearances and pain, we are accompanied by a God who loves us.

You can't surrender to someone you don't know. You can't surrender because surrender requires trust. How can you trust someone you don't know? And how can you get to know someone you don't spend time with? We will explore this further in the next chapter.

CHAPTER 6

The Heart Without a Secret Place

He that dwelleth in the secret place of the Most High shall abide under the shadow of the Almighty. Psalm 91:1, KJV

My family has land overlooking a well-known river in northwest Oklahoma. You've got to drive over some rough pasture to get there, but once you do, the view is breathtaking. Standing on the edge of the "bluff," as us Okies call it, you can look out and see for miles. The blue sky illuminates the green trees, and it causes the murky undertones of the Cimarron River to dance with intensity—as if someone has placed a disco ball in the water. The view is expansive, even on a cloudy day.

When it's quiet, you can hear coyotes yipping, birds chirping, and cows calling for their babies. If you dare to look down, you'll see the jagged edge of the rock kissing the ground where tracks of wildlife have passed by the old cars that line the banks.

This is my favorite place to visit, for many reasons. I grew up going to "The Bluffs" with my grandpa, whom I lovingly referred to as "Pabo." We had many conversations about life and cattle. He imparted wisdom into my life, and I added joy to his. After we lost him to cancer, I would go up there to feel like I was closer to heaven, and therefore, closer to him. I would remember many conversations we had, and my heart began to heal. It's also where my husband proposed to me one cold January evening. He took me under the guise we were going coyote hunting, but instead, took me up on the bluffs and asked me to be his wife.

This is my physical "secret place." My family knows about it, and people have seen pictures, but not many know where it is or how to get there. It's where I go when I need a moment to breathe, need a reminder of God's goodness, or when I need to revisit a conversation to grasp a nugget of Pabo's wisdom. It's where everything comes to life for me.

In Matthew 6:6, Jesus instructs us to go to a quiet place, shut the door, and pray. It's not so much about a hidden physical location as it is a place where you can go to meet with God one-on-one. We learn more about God, and He transforms us to become more like Him.

I love the story of David. In men's eyes, he was the least obvious choice for king, but he was the man God wanted to use to bring His plan on earth to pass. David was a shepherd boy. Now, I know there are some things left to the imagination concerning Scripture, like what David did while he was out in the field with the sheep. Did he count them? Talk to them? Spend time with God? We don't know because the Bible doesn't say. However, to me, this is a great example of the "secret place," and to show you how, we need to jump forward a bit in David's life.

David had brothers who followed King Saul into war against the Philistines. While his brothers were at war, Jesse, David's father, sent him to take food to the camp where his brothers were staying. Upon David's arrival to the battle lines to greet his brothers, a Philistine by the name of Goliath rose to defy the army of Israel.

Seemingly, this perturbed David because he asked, "What will be done for the man who kills this Philistine and removes this disgrace from Israel? Who is this uncircumcised Philistine that he should defy the armies of the living God?" (1 Samuel 17:26 NIV).

David knew Israel was God's chosen people, and he knew whoever defied Israel defied God. He didn't see a giant who was capable of putting the hurt on an army, but he saw someone who was coming against what God was doing. The story goes on to tell of David approaching Saul, telling him he would go and fight this giant. Saul tries to tell him he isn't capable of doing it, but David would not believe it.

But David said to Saul, 'Your servant has been keeping his father's sheep. When a lion or a bear came and carried off a sheep from the flock, I went after it, struck it, and rescued the sheep from its mouth. When it turned on me, I seized it by its hair, struck it and killed it. Your servant has killed both the lion and the bear; this uncircumcised Philistine will be like one of them, because he defied the armies of the living God. The Lord who rescued me from the paw of the lion and the paw of the bear will rescue me from the hand of this Philistine.' (1 Samuel 17:34-37, NIV)

David knew nothing but God's faithfulness to protect His people. Where did this knowledge and confidence come from?

By spending time with God. David was mentioned as a man after God's own heart. Anyone familiar with David knew he didn't live a perfect life, but he lived a life seeking the heart of God. I believe David became that man after God's own heart when he was a boy.

Before David defeated Goliath, the Prophet Samuel was instructed to go and anoint someone else as king because God had rejected Saul for being disobedient. The Prophet Samuel went to the house of Jesse and saw Jesse's eldest son, Eliab. Upon first impression, Samuel thought he would be a perfect fit for the next king. However, God had something else in mind.

In 1 Samuel 16:7, the Lord says to Samuel, 'Do not consider his appearance or his height, for I have rejected him. The Lord does not look at the things people look at. People look at the outward appearance, but the Lord looks at the heart'" (NIV).

After going through each son and still not finding what he was looking for, Samuel asked Jesse if he had more sons. Jesse sent for the youngest, David, and upon David's arrival, the Lord told Samuel he was the one to anoint. Even after David's anointing, he returned to tend to his father's sheep. His return to care for the sheep had taught him an important thing he needed to know to defeat Goliath: authority.

I imagine those moments in the field were some of the most intimate times with the Lord David experienced. In the years preceding the time David became King, there were trials David had to endure that would cause any of us to wonder if what had taken place was real or imagined.

When he was invited to play music for King Saul, he could have easily believed it was his moment to be King. When Saul began trying to kill him, he could have become discouraged and wondered if Saul would succeed. I like to think David often returned to a field to meet with God and cry out to Him for strength and wisdom.

Intimacy with Father God isn't found in a well-sung worship song. It's not found in a sermon that makes you shout, "Amen!" It's not found in goosebumps, and it's not found when you stand on a platform and preach a message that saves hundreds. Intimacy with God is found in the secret place. Intimacy is choosing Him and desiring Him over all else: over your circumstances, over your fears, and over your doubts. It's digging deep, kneeling to receive strength from Him when you want to give up.

Intimacy is created by spending time with Him in the secret place: His presence.

We all have intimate relationships, whether it is with a spouse, a family member, or a friend. Intimacy isn't only physical; it's a deep emotional connection binding two people together. Intimacy is connection with someone you share all your secrets with, all your worries, concerns, dreams, and fears. That intimacy is reciprocated as they share those same things with you. It's a deep trust, knowing that person isn't going to betray you.

When my husband and I first began dating, we had conversations that would have made others run for the hills. We shared the deepest place of our hearts with one another. It was the first conversation in which I knew he would be the one I married. Why? Because I trusted him with my heart, and he trusted me with his.

It is no different with Father God. He desires an intimate relationship with each one of us so He can share what is on His heart. He doesn't want to keep things from us but rather teach us how to live through quiet, intimate time with Him. The secret place is a place where you begin to take God at His word and trust Him for who He is.

When was the last time you allowed yourself to be deeply loved by God? When was the last time you shut the door to your closet and spent one-on-one time with Him, listening to what He is saying to you?

Too many times we settle for the last servings spiritually. We feed everyone else, making sure they are nourished, but we neglect our own nourishment until the end, which often results in no nourishment. Feeding others isn't wrong, but the order in which we do it needs to be addressed and changed. We cannot spiritually feed others from our spiritual emptiness. If we are empty because we feed others first, we begin to seek fulfillment in other areas. However, if we feed ourselves first, then others, we will not feast on the things of this world because we are filled with the things of God.

How are you feeding yourself? How are you allowing yourself to be nourished?

You are God's child *first* before you are a father, mother, daughter, grandmother, aunt, business owner, wife, pastor, teacher, leader, ministry worker, or volunteer. Whatever your title is, whatever you do, and the effectiveness of it flows from being His child *first*.

His will is not that we pour from an empty cup and carry burdens too heavy for us. In Matthew 11, Jesus tells us His yoke is easy and His burden is light. All of us are in different seasons requiring something of us. No matter the season, it is crucial we establish a "first" with God. "First" is exactly how it sounds: giving God the first of everything. The first of your time, the first of your day, the first of your thoughts.

I would bet I could guess your thoughts.

You don't know what season I'm in, Tay. I am exhausted and run down.

Perfect. Come to the Father, *first*. It is not impossible to do, regardless of the season you are in. Jesus was a great example of this. In Mark 1, we read of Jesus rising early and going to an isolated place to pray. He was giving Father God the first of His day. Jesus, we know, was consistently busy from the time people gathered around Him until the end of the day. The ministry of Jesus flowed from His time with the Father.

Did you know it is God's desire to tell us what He is doing?

No longer do I call you servants, for the servant does not know what his master is doing; but I have called you friends, for all that I have heard from my Father I have made known to you. (John 15:15, ESV)

There's a condition to it, however. That condition is abiding with Him. Dwelling with Him in the secret place. The word "remain" or "abide," is mentioned in John 15 eleven times.

The Greek word for "remain" is the word "meno," which means "to abide, remain." I love what Bible scholar Ruckert Abendmahl says about remaining:

"Something has established itself permanently within my soul, and always exerts its power in me."[10]

The power in abiding with God not only works as a driving force, but it is the foundation for everything else. I took a shop class in high school where I learned about various woodworking skills, as well as other construction projects. The foundation of projects was imperative to the success of many of my projects, and it is no different in the construction of a house.

The main purpose of a foundation is to make the structure firm and to keep ground moisture from seeping in and weakening the home. If you do not have a firm foundation, you do not have a firm structure, and anything is able to take it out. There are times foundations go bad and need to be repaired and replaced.

Remaining with God is foundation building time. It is where His presence establishes its permanence within us, so that no matter what we do, He always exerts His power in us.

It's not about us and what we can do. It's not about our net worth or how successful we are. It's not about how big our business or ministry is. It's about intimacy with the Father. It's why He sent His only Son to die on the cross for our sins. Every blessing we receive is a bonus flowing from a relationship with Him. We had been separated from Him by sin, and He so desired a connection with us once more, He made a sacrifice once and for all: Jesus.

CHAPTER 7

Building a Heart of Humility

In the movie *Spider-Man: Homecoming*, the powers Peter Parker had been given was noticed by the head Avenger: Iron Man, Tony Stark. This was a big deal because Peter was just a boy and still in school. Tony though, recognizing his talent, knew Peter needed time to develop and prepare before he would be ready for larger endeavors, so he asked Peter to become the "friendly neighborhood Spider-Man." Seeing it as a blow and feeling he was ready for the big stuff because Tony had recognized him, Peter decided to disregard Tony's command and do as he pleased.

In his disobedience, Peter came across an illegal firearms deal. He attempted to stop the deal and failed at the task. He took the information he saw back to Tony Stark, who told him to leave it alone. Peter believed Tony was writing him off and was upset he wasn't being taken seriously.

The second encounter Spider-Man had with the illegal firearms dealer took place on a ferry. Spider-Man knew of the meeting details from his previous encounter with the criminal and decided he would end it himself since no one else seemed to care about it. During the firefight that develops, one of the weapons burned right down through the middle of the ferry, causing it to split apart, and putting the lives of those on the ferry in danger.

Realizing the problem, Spider-Man went back and forth between the two pieces of the ferry using his web to piece it back together, but in his rushing, he missed a spot. His web could no longer hold the boat. It began to break and chaos ensued. When all hope seemed to be lost, Iron Man, Tony Stark, arrived on scene and saved the day.

Not only was this a picture of disobedience and pride and the repercussions of both, but the conversation that took place between Peter and Tony was convicting.

Tony meets Peter on top of a building to hash out what happened. In the midst of the conversation, Tony tells Peter he needs his Spider-Man outfit back. Peter asks for how long, and Tony tells him forever.

"I'm nothing without this suit," Peter tells Tony.

"If you're nothing without the suit, then you shouldn't have it."[11]

Pride tells us we deserve a certain accolade or position, and we're nothing without it. The potential of success gets to our heads, and we begin to separate ourselves from the "lower position" because of where we believe we are headed. Humility says it's God who places us in positions of prominence and influence, and God can also remove us from those places of prominence and influence.

Humility is key in growing into what it is God has called you to do. There is no room for pride in the kingdom of God.

Can I ask you a question?

Even if every promise you believe God has spoken to you does not come to pass, would you still follow Him? If nothing happened, would you bow to the things of this world and render God unfaithful? God is not unfaithful; let me say that right now. He is faithful to His word, and when something lines up according to His word, it will come to pass. But I believe the previous questions we must continually ask ourselves because our answer will reveal our spiritual maturity and our motive for following Christ.

In the book of Daniel, three men were faced with losing their lives unless they bowed to the king and worshipped him and his golden image. Instead of bowing, they told him they weren't going to bow, because they believed God would save them.

But even if he does not, we want you to know, Your Majesty, that we will not serve your gods or worship the image of gold you have set up. (Daniel 3:18, NIV)

I struggled with this phrase, "*even if he does not...*" I saw it as a form of doubt. I was of the mindset God could not fail and nothing bad would ever happen to those who followed Him, and reading this passage challenged that theology in me. I wanted to believe He wouldn't dare let them perish. I didn't want to have a shred of doubt in His promises. But, this isn't about doubt. It's about faith and trust in Him and what He has called us to carry out.

It's about whether or not we will choose Him, even when everything seems to be against us. We are willing to celebrate our successes, and trust Him when all is going well, but are we willing to withstand those things that come against us to reach what God has for us?

We live in a fallen world. We will face trouble. We will face what is contrary to God's word and His character, but will we trust His character, or will we say, "I guess you don't want this for me," and walk away?

Even if He doesn't heal me this side of heaven, will I still follow Him?
Even if He doesn't provide this financially, will I still choose Him?
Even if my dreams don't come to pass like I believed they would, will I still follow Him?

Do I personally believe His will and His desire is to heal? Above all else.
Do I believe it's His will and desire we prosper? Above all else.
Do I believe His plans for us are for good and not harm and I have a purpose? Above all else.

The process determines whether or not we are in this for the long haul, come hell or high water. There's more to it than the victory, and to reach the victory, we have to endure the battle. Sometimes the battle causes us to question His goodness, but remember this: you can have faith and still say "even if."

When you say "even if," it doesn't negate His goodness nor His word. Even if He doesn't do it in the way we think He should, following Him is still greater than anything this world has to offer.

Imagine the following: you have just been invited to a seat at the table of the President of the United States, or the Queen of England, whichever you prefer. Chances are, they don't know you personally, but the invitation was extended to you. When you arrive at the party, you see there doesn't seem to be any name plates indicating specific seats, so you take a seat wherever you'd like.

Where would you sit and why? Do you sit where this person of prominence can see you and hopefully talk to you, or do you take a seat down the table, honored to even be in the presence of this person?

There is a similar story to the one above in the Bible, found in Luke 14. Jesus was at the home of a prominent Pharisee. There was a man with dropsy Jesus had healed, and though the healing was a magnificent thing, Jesus noticed those in attendance were not focused on the miracle that took place but their position in the place of prominence. Let's look at the scene in Luke 14:

When he noticed how the guests picked the places of honor at the table, he told them this parable: 'When someone invites you to a wedding feast, do not take the place of honor, for a person more distinguished than you may have been invited.
(Luke 14:7-8, NIV)

Jesus goes on to tell the guests if someone more distinguished shows up, those who picked the places of honor will be asked to move. Generally speaking, many seats would be full, so it would be likely the person who sat in the place of honor would have to walk past everyone else to a seat at the end of the table.

Jesus goes on to say if you seat yourself in the seat of "least important," and you are the distinguished guest, you will be asked to move up to a place of honor. He ends with this:

For all those who exalt themselves will be humbled, and those who humble themselves will be exalted. (Luke 14:11, NIV)

What place are you giving yourself? It doesn't matter what position you have, if you place yourself above anyone else, you can guarantee you will tumble under them.

As a society, we have become so "me" focused. We feel in order to be offered a position or feel important, we have to put ourselves in positions of honor so as not to be overlooked.

Let me tell you: God can put your name on the minds and in the mouths of people of prominence to give you a higher position, *without* your help. It's true. I've had it happen. I've found myself the subject of conversations without even knowing the people who were talking about me, and these conversations resulted in a position I didn't realize was available.

Not to mention, the less time you spend trying to put yourself in a place of influence and the more you remain faithful where you are, the more likely you will stand out head and shoulders above those who are fighting for a position.

Regardless of whether or not you think you deserve a place of honor, Christians are called to choose the place of humility and submission before God. It's not the loudest person who receives a place of honor, but the one who is humble. I'm not saying to do these things so that you get a place of honor. If you are more focused on the recognition than the condition of your heart, it's time to examine where your focus lies.

Remaining in a constant state of being teachable means we understand that we don't know all there is to know. As part of the body of Christ, we need each other to help us grow and mature to walk in the fullness of our calling. When we walk in humility, it's revealed that we're willing to learn from God's word and live a life that reflects His love.

Humility is a willingness to be used by God, pursued by God, and molded by God. It is laying yourself down and choosing what pleases Him. It's a constant altar call—a choice to always change and prepare to be used by Him. Humility is answering the call to be sensitive to the Holy Spirit. It isn't about maintaining a certain status, but maintaining a willingness to serve, love, and honor those around you.

CHAPTER 8

Building a Heart of Integrity

In March of 2019, I quit my full-time job of less than a year to go back home and prepare for what God had next for me. I had no idea what the "next" was, but I knew better than to disobey, so I turned in my two weeks notice.

The paragraph above describes the pattern of my life over the last eight years. I have been in that position before. In fact, I was in that position before I took the job. I was building my brand, preparing courses, writing blogs, and studying when I felt like God was asking me to take my last job. I learned such valuable information while there: how to persist, work past the "no," be sensitive to the Holy Spirit, love people, and use business as a ministry.

It started when I was at a women's conference and felt the call of God to transform lives through writing and speaking. I was tired of chasing what I thought would fill me and decided to fully surrender to the work God wanted to do in my life, no matter what it looked like.

The last eight years have been a test of my integrity. I have taken opportunities that have wasted precious time doing things where I wasn't growing my gifts.

In 1 Corinthians 9:27, Paul tells us people don't enter into a race without strict training in advance (paraphrased). Other versions say athletes are self-controlled in the things they do. We see Olympic athletes at the tail end of their season of preparing and disciplining themselves. We don't see the hours and days of sacrifice and self-discipline they carry out to get to that point. The Olympics is the end result of months and years of dedication.

From strength training to sleep habits, recovery and diet, it takes years of discipline to get where their bodies can handle the intensity of the Olympics. *Forbes* released an article in 2008 stating Olympic athletes train for *four to eight years*[12] before they make it to the Olympics. They set goals in advance that they work toward.

NBA players, PGA golfers, NFL players, professional rodeo athletes—they get to those positions through self-discipline. While everyone else is choosing to do whatever they want, these athletes are choosing to do things that propel them in their arena of success.

It is no different for us as Christians or even as people aspiring to succeed. Everything we do, whether good or bad, great or small, all adds up to the greater things we choose to do and what happens as a result.

My question to you is: what are you doing when you're not being watched? Are you putting the right things into your body to be able to run the race? Are you putting the right things into your mind so you can pass the test for licensing? Are you reading up on how to design a website and marketing tools so you can take your business to the next level?

I want to go a little deeper, and I want to test your foundation. What is your motive? What is your intent with acceleration? Is it self-promotion? Is it to glorify God?

Think about those who built the Tower of Babel. Their intent was to build a tower that went up to the heavens so others would see and be impressed with what they had accomplished. That is pride, and it's a tactic of the enemy, who was thrown out of Heaven because of misplaced worship. The Tower of Babel was destroyed because of misplaced worship. Confusion is always the result of pride and idolatry—we seek to find the answers in other areas that deepen the idolatry of self.

I don't think the Tower of Babel being built was necessarily wrong in the sense of building something large, but I believe what was wrong was the intent of self-promotion in building it.

According to *Encyclopedia Britannica*[13], Babylonia, where the Tower of Babel was built, was the land of Shinar, where people settled. Babylonia was known for a place of prostitution and idolatry—misplaced intimacy and worship.

It's easy to get caught up in making a name for ourselves or building a following. If you look at the business principles of success, at the root of success is promotion: getting your stuff out there for everyone to see so everyone knows who you are and what you do. I think of people who have created a name for themselves in the area of wealth. Where I'm from, people are land rich. There are two types of people: those who own a lot of land and those who have a lot of land *and* a lot of money. Conversations are usually peppered with certain names who donated money and how much money to a certain cause or organization. I've known people with money say they don't need God as long as they have financial resources. I've seen wealth and the desire for wealth make people do crazy things.

The Tower of Babel was built out of insecurity and fear. They didn't want to be spread out over all of the earth, and moving away would mean they were cutting ties with their legacy and wouldn't be remembered. They wanted to create a place of refuge where people knew their greatness. There is nothing wrong with creating a legacy or being remembered. God told Abraham and David He would make their name great. However, there's a difference in creating your own legacy and walking in the one God has created for you.

In ancient days, the Tower of Babel would have probably been a ziggurat. A ziggurat resembles a pyramid, but I was floored by the difference. A ziggurat may resemble something great on the outside, like a pyramid, but there is *nothing* on the inside.

Think about it. How many times have we focused on our outside appearance, what people see immediately, but we take no effort to fill the inside with good? It's an empty platform. Everyone is wanting to do something new and create great things, and the way of the world is to create a brand and an awareness of our product and who we are. How many of us are building empty platforms because we're too wrapped up in creating an appearance we think will outlast us?

Matthew 15:18 tells us what is inside of us is what will come out (paraphrased). If our inside is empty with no sustenance, then what we do will be flawed, and what will be produced is more emptiness. But, if we allow ourselves to be filled with God, if we take time to invest in our relationship with Him, what we create will be what fills other's lives with God's goodness. From the beginning, the command was to be fruitful and multiply. But, if we're producing from emptiness, we're going to produce and multiply emptiness. This will cause people to continue searching aimlessly for the fulfillment our hearts were meant to experience. If we are fruitful and multiply from a place of relationship with God, what we produce will lead others to the only thing that fulfills- a relationship with Christ.

When we are too busy making ourselves known, we will forget God has already promised to make our name great. Here is something that is so neat to me.

In Genesis 12, God tells Abram He will make his name great.

I will make you into a great nation, and I will bless you; I will make your name great, and you will be a blessing.
(ESV)

God told Abram it would be Him who would make his name great. Check out the next chapter. Abram and his family became so wealthy in land and livestock that the land they were on *could not support them*. Are you seeing this? The same thing the people who built the Tower of Babel wanted to accomplish, God was doing for Abram. Isn't it the goodness of God to tell Abram what He would do for him? It's like He was saying,

"I want to do all these things through you, but you have to trust Me." Abraham never tried to elevate himself. Don't get me started on the descendants of Abraham! God knew how important a legacy was, so He set out to bless Abraham as he trusted in Him.

We don't need more fame or fortune. We don't need more Instagram followers or Facebook likes. We don't have to post on social media at the right time to guarantee maximum exposure. We don't need any of that.

Matthew 6:33 tells us to seek His Kingdom first and all we need will be added to us (paraphrased).

It's not our business plan that attracts success; it's not the number of sales or the number of people sitting in church on Sunday. It's the presence of God. It's His Holy Spirit. We don't need more money, we need more of the Holy Spirit. Why? Because the Holy Spirit is God, and He is our power from on high. When we have more of the Holy Spirit, we will have the things we need.

We say, "I need more money," or, "I need a better job," or, "I need marriage counseling," and I'm not saying you don't need those things, but what you need is *the Holy Spirit*. When was the last time something happened and your first thought was to cry out in prayer, "Father, I need more of Your Holy Spirit."

I am so convicted by this. There have been *many* times, even recently, where I have said, "I need money before I can step out and do what I feel God is calling me to do." While that is the truth, money is not the first and only thing I need. I have it backwards. I have been so focused on the material things, I have not sought His Kingdom first, and then all I need will be added to me.

We don't need better business plans, we need more of the Holy Spirit, because without the Holy Spirit, we're just a bunch of ziggurats: displaying the appearance of power on the outside but empty on the inside.

CHAPTER 9

The Fully Persuaded Heart

I cannot count the number of times I have wanted to quit the journey of fulfilling what God has called me to do. I have hit mental roadblocks observing the way others were successful, trying it their way, and ending up in more confusion. I have felt frustration because it seemed I had no blueprint to follow, but when there were blueprints, there seemed to be too many to decide which was the right one.

So, how do we deal with the emotions we face on the journey from anointing to appointing? What do we do when we come up against no blueprint or too many blueprints? I've discovered it comes down to one question:

Will you go to the battle lines for what God has called you to do, or will you shrink back in fear and question whether or not He really called you to this life?

Not only does this pertain to what we feel God has called us to do, but it pertains to our walk with Him. Are you confident God's promises are for you? Will you stand on the battlefront with bullets flying at you, accusations and slander, confusion and chaos, whatever it may be; will you stand and fight and declare the promises of God? Or will you shrink back in fear because you're suddenly unsure what He says is true?

What is the status of your faith in receiving what God has promised? Are you fully persuaded and unwavering? Are you confident but waver occasionally? Or, do you want to be sure but find yourself tossed around by winds of doubt and confusion?

It is easy to allow the landscape of what's in front of us to obscure the view we had in faith. There are times the promise of God for your life seems so far away you wonder if you were daydreaming the moment you knew He called you. Other times, the promise you received seems so close you can taste it.

The time between the moment I knew God called me to write and speak to when I truly began walking in a portion of that calling was nine years.

Over the last nine years, my life has looked like devouring His Scriptures for promises concerning my calling and declaring those promises over my life. It has looked like being stripped of selfish motives, fear, doubt, and confusion. It looked like being hidden so others can't see my God-given talents until He opens the door. It has looked like obedience. Obedience made me look like I had lost my mind, while I simultaneously felt like I had lost my mind but was too proud to admit it or do something different.

There have been times over the last nine years I was giving God an ultimatum because the landscape before me seemed empty and fruitless. I was counting on His provision to make it through the week. I have been put in positions financially over the last nine years that tested my faith and my sanity, especially when it involved two of us living on one income. When He told me to quit my job and stay home to write, not just once but twice, I fought it because nothing tangibly significant happened the last time I did it. There was no breakthrough in my writing. No publishing deal for a book, no speaking opportunities, nothing. Instead, what seemed to happen was financial strain, confusion about whether or not I was trying to make it happen in my time, and frustration because I felt like it was my fault we were in the position we were in.

I haven't wavered in faith concerning what He has called me to do, but I have wavered in faith concerning the path He has taken me on. I've mostly wavered in the area of wondering whether or not I heard Him correctly for the next step.

We have to be unwavering in our faith, no matter how hard it gets. We have to continue to contend for the promises of God, despite the amount of time it's been between the promise and the manifestation.

Abraham was given a promise that took twenty-five years to come to pass. Joseph was given dreams that took thirteen years to come to pass. David was anointed king still a shepherd boy while Saul was still king.

In each of these instances, these men were given a promise of something to come, but each of them faced opposition that could have caused them to quit. Paul was thrown into prison, where he penned much of the New Testament. He could have quit, thinking since he was in prison, God had forgotten him. Esther risked her life to go before King Ahaseurus to plead for the lives of the Jewish nation. Instead of bowing to fear, she rose up in faith, trusting that God would give her favor before the King. Everyone I mentioned endured until the end. So, what gives?

They were fully persuaded God would do as He said. No matter the opposition they faced, they believed God would make good on His promises.

Opposition is hard. It causes you to question whether or not you were supposed to do something. It is unfortunate because it seems in today's society, there is no perseverance. At the start of any level of opposition, people often shut down and quit because it is too hard. I've even heard in the Christian circle, "Maybe I'm not supposed to do this," when people come up against opposition.

Sometimes opposition is there to divert us from what God has called us to do, and other times, opposition is there to protect us or redirect us to a better way. Not all opposition is there to tell us we aren't in the right place. Sometimes opposition tests us to see what our grit factor is. Will we push past and keep standing on God's promises, or will we quit because it's too much?

It is difficult when you feel you are given a promise and it seems everything *except* that promise is happening. In fact, it seems like you are going in the opposite direction than you had initially planned. How do you keep standing, and even keep walking, toward that promise without losing hope? I mean,

David was *pursued* by Saul to be killed. He can't be King if he is dead! But if he wasn't prepared in the field first, if he didn't have to endure, and he was immediately made king, who is to say he would have been able to defeat Goliath and stand up to Saul? More importantly, he defeated Goliath because he knew God had equipped him for that exact moment by killing the lion and the bear.

Opposition can come in the form of hardship or delay. Whatever form it takes, are you persuaded? Are you persuaded God has seen that opposition and is making a way? Are you persuaded a minor set-back is an opportunity to grow and learn? Are you persuaded that you convince your mind by speaking His promise out loud over yourself? What comes out of your mouth when opposition arises?

Oftentimes, we see preparation time as opposition, and we try to rebuke the situation, when in reality, God may be wanting to deal with whatever issue is at hand. Preparation time is never wasted time because it creates a more solid foundation within us. There are things within us that are contrary to the word and the character of God that need to be removed so we can live our life in the fullness of His calling and bring Him glory, growing closer to Him.

We can be fully persuaded in what He has called us to do and not be fully persuaded that He's going to come through. We can be fully persuaded He will come through but not in what He's called us to do. But how do we become fully persuaded in both?

By trusting Him. Trust is a lot like love in that it's not based on a feeling, but action. Even if you don't feel like trusting, you do it anyway because you know He is good. You act on that trust by speaking what His word says about you and your situation. You act on it by choosing to trust Him despite what is in front of you.

The enemy always speaks the opposite of what is actually happening, and it's easier to believe what he is saying because it's within the grasp of our eyesight: we see our circumstances are still the same, the anxiety is still there, and the relationship is still strained.

You hear you can't go on anymore; your story isn't worth telling because people won't listen. You hear you're not worthy of a seat at the table, or your situation won't change. You hear it's another lap around the mountain, and you really weren't set free because you're not good enough.

But here's the thing: every area of conquest has an enemy that won't give up the position. It's not a breakthrough without a battle to defeat the enemy. Throughout the Bible are accounts of people standing at the brink of their promise with enemies defending the territory.

Take the twelve spies, for example. They were sent to spy on their Promised Land. Ten came back and said there were giants in the land, and they were unable to defeat them.

I love what Exodus 23 says:

I will send my terror ahead of you and throw into confusion every nation you encounter. I will make all of your enemies turn their backs and run. I will send the hornet ahead of you to drive out the Hivites, Canaanites, and Hittites out of your way. But I will not drive them out in a single year, because the land would become desolate and the wild animals too numerous for you. Little by little, I will drive them out before you until you have increased enough to take possession of the land. (Exodus 23:27-30, NIV)

God is not a God of overwhelming defeat; He is a God of overwhelming victory. He is not going to drive out all of our enemies at once because we would not know how to defeat them. We cannot defeat our enemies at once, no matter how capable we think we are. There were times throughout various journeys I was on I thought, "I just want to be done. I want to be at the end of this, with the prize in hand." To me, it would have been easier, but I didn't know what I would encounter along the way that would show me what I needed to know to take hold of the Promised Land.

Had God run all of my enemies out of the way, I wouldn't have learned how much I needed Him to sustain me. I wouldn't have wanted His presence so much I could feel it in my bones. I would not have learned who I was in Him or how to trust or be bold and overcome the enemy. I wouldn't have seen God go to bat for me and drive the enemy from me. It wasn't me defeating the enemy; it was taking God at His word and watching Him pave the way for me to keep walking.

We do not know what is up ahead. Again, anything promised is worth defending, and the enemy knows the power of God's promises, so he will do all he can to keep us from that promise. He isn't standing at the gates awaiting our arrival to say, "I've been keeping this for you." No, he knows you're coming, so he does all he can to keep you *from* God's promises. He knows your possession of God's promise equals his failure and his defeat. Let's revisit what God says in verse 30.

Little by little, I will drive them out before you, until you have
increased enough to take possession of the land.
(Exodus 23:30, NIV)

Underline that last part, *"until you have increased enough to*
take possession of the land."

Small victories add up until we enter our Promised Land. What do you do on those days where you feel you're barely scraping by, those days where you have to dig deep to keep going, and those days you worship because your thoughts are overwhelming you to the point you need someone else to tell you what to say? Take heart and remember that those days are victories that are causing you to increase so you can take possession of the promise. You may not see the increase, or feel victorious, but you will look back months down the road and see the forward motion you have made. God knows the amount you can handle, and it's different from what we think. The phrase 'God gives His toughest battles to His strongest soldiers' is good in theory, but sometimes, the battle is too much, so we quit taking matters into our own hands and let Him fight on our behalf.

If you don't come up to an obstacle and feel the pressure to get around it, you won't. Sometimes, we have to endure the pressure because of the increase waiting on the other side.

Let's continue in Exodus 23.

I will establish your borders from the Red Sea to the
Mediterranean and from the desert to the Euphrates River.
And I will give into your hands the people who live in the
land and you will drive them out before you. Do not make a
covenant with them or with their gods. Do not let them live in
your land or they will cause you to sin against me, because
the worship of their gods will certainly be a snare to you.
(Exodus 23:31-33, NIV)

God saw ahead the landmines of the battlefield and warned the
Israelites of what was to come. If defeating the enemies before
them were going to be easy, He wouldn't have made a point to
warn them of what might happen. It's hard to stand our ground
when we have people and situations coming against our faith.
We will want to give in to those people or situations at times,
but when we refuse to allow ourselves to make a covenant
with those situations that arise, and we instead choose to take
Him at His word and trust Him, the enemy is defeated because
we're not allowing him to dictate our response to the situation.
Strength and faith arise when we see the situation and instead
declare He is God and His Word says He will take care of us.
We can't ignore the jaunts of the enemy, thinking they'll go
away. We have to come against his words with our words of
faith in Christ to defeat the enemy in the land to which God
has called us.

Therefore, since through God's mercy we have this ministry,
we do not lose heart. Rather, we have renounced secret and
shameful ways; we do not use deception, nor do we distort
the word of God. On the contrary, by setting forth the truth

*plainly, we commend ourselves to everyone's conscience in
the sight of God.* (2 Corinthians 4:1-2, NIV)

It's not "our" ministry, but it has been given to us by God's
mercy. What God has called you to is from Him and He will
use it, or He wouldn't have called you to it. Don't lose heart.
Jesus was staring at the pinnacle of the reason he came, and
the enemy knew it. He knew if he could get Jesus to agree with
his twisted truths, God's plan through him would be thwarted.
Satan tempted Jesus with misplaced worship by offering Jesus
what He would have through carrying out the intended plan
of God: all the kingdoms of the world. But because of Jesus'
lifelong obedience to God, the enemy's camp was overturned.

There will be times when we are trusting God to complete in us
what He started so we can see an "overview" of where He has
called us to impact. There will be opportunities and temptations
to obtain the promise by force instead of obedience. But what
you obtain by force, you have to keep by force. We are His
witnesses and in order to accurately represent Him, we must
go through a time of pruning, or threshing, or winnowing, to
remove what doesn't witness to His character, so it can be
replaced with what accurately represents Him. Not only that,
but so we can experience intimacy with Him.

When we choose to fight from a position of faith by trusting
Him, we are recognizing His ways are higher than our ways
and His thoughts higher than our thoughts. Not only that, but
instead of saying, "God has a purpose for the pain," we declare
His word of faith over the situation. Why?

As the rain and the snow come down from heaven, and do

not return to it without watering the earth and making it bud and flourish, so that it yields seed for the sower and bread for the eater, so is my word that goes out from my mouth: It will not return to me empty, but will accomplish what I desire and achieve the purpose for which I sent it.
(Isaiah 55:10-11, NIV)

His Word always accomplishes what it says it will do. It's not an empty threat or command. Jeremiah 1:12 tells us He watches over His Word to perform it (paraphrased). When we speak His Word to the mountain of our situation, we are applying the Word that has been spoken from the beginning of time, and it's accomplishing the purpose for which it was sent. Not only that, but when we speak His Words, we are tearing down the strongholds and the systems the enemy has resurrected against us and we are re-establishing His kingdom on earth in our lives.

Do not lose heart in where God has you. Speak His Word over the situation that is contrary to what you see going on in life. Seek His face and trust Him because everything is for a greater purpose than you. Trust Him in the process and see how He is pruning you to carry out what He has called you to. Do not fear. He has anointed you for the position, but you must learn the landscape before you're appointed into that place. He is growing you into who He has already created you to be. He has assigned you to the place He has called you, and He will move mountains and do the impossible to place you where you need to be, but you have to trust Him.

CHAPTER 10

The Pioneering Heart

I believe God is doing a new thing and has been doing a new thing for quite some time. This new thing is unlike anything we've ever seen before on this Earth. I believe there is a level of awakening taking place that not only awakens people to their destinies, but ushers in a revival we've not yet seen. It takes stewards to bring that forth. People who are willing to go the distance and, regardless of the cost, carry His kingdom agenda out on the Earth. I believe there are pioneers who have been called to steward the new thing God is doing, and you, my friend, are a pioneer.

Pioneering is hard. It is flat out difficult, and at times, discouraging. I'm not trying to scare you, but I don't want you to think pioneering is all rainbows and butterflies because there are times when it's the opposite: cloudy days and stink bugs.

You will come up against some of the hardest moments of your life in the journey from anointing to appointing. Moments won't make sense, circumstances will look completely opposite of what you believe God has spoken, confusion will be utterly convincing at times, and you will feel stuck in the tension between tenacity and throwing in the towel.

There will be well-meaning people who will try and "stabilize" you for the sake of normalcy and security. They don't want to see you fail. But here's something I want you to know: failure isn't final when we serve the God of triumph. Will you fail? Yup. You'll hear wrong, you'll move too fast, not move fast enough, you'll miss it at times. You name it, you'll probably do it.

The good news is God always forgives, always redeems, and always leads. When you're sensitive and obedient to Him, even when you miss it, He will reroute you. Don't allow others to uproot what God has planted within you though. Some may say it's impossible, but You were made to step out and do what you have been placed on Earth to do. By you, others may come to know God and see their God-sized dreams are possible too.

Moving forward doesn't come automatically. It is a choice. A daily choice. It's an ebb and flow of moments and emotions that require your decision to stick it out no matter how hard it gets or who says you're crazy. Pioneering will test your tenacity and willpower. It'll test your obedience and your honor. Sometimes, it'll feel like it's testing your sanity.

You will experience loneliness. People won't understand why you are making the decisions you are or why you're walking out the very definition of insanity. Though it's the world's definition of insanity, it's God's definition of faith. You will have to do the same thing over and over, sometimes with no immediate results, sometimes with immediate results, and sometimes as a simple act of obedience that breaks doors wide open elsewhere.

We are made in God's image. Built into each one of us is the knowledge of God and a knowing of our Creator. We might not know it mentally, but we know it deep within our spirits. Anything that comes up against the natural design of God's image within us is a battle taking place. If someone calls us a name or says something contrary to the design of God, we *feel* it deep within us. It hurts, it causes confusion, it causes us to try and overcome in a way to prove someone wrong.

Why is that? It's because we *know* it's not the truth, even if we haven't read it in His Word or had a revealed knowledge of it. It's like the feeling you have when you *know* you were made for more but you don't know what it is.

I have struggled greatly with branding, finding a niche, and marketing. It's not because I think they're bad. I do believe you can self-promote, but I also know there is a way to promote the message God has given you without promoting yourself. Where I have struggled is finding where I fit in. In my journey from anointing to appointing, the Holy Spirit has been revealing to me what it is I'm pioneering. I don't know the exact details; all I know is I'm paving a way for others to come behind me as I do what God has called them to do.

When we receive a promise from God, there will be things that test our commitment to God. Are we going to call it quits, saying He's not faithful, or we didn't hear correctly, or He was lying? Or are we going to dig in deep, realizing the opposition we're facing now will only result in a greater and closer relationship with God? Are we going to draw near to

Him, trusting He is good, and His Word is good? Are we going to take back the words and vows we said when we surrendered to Him? Will we use our authority we were given and speak the name of Jesus to change our situation and command only God to have the rightful inheritance to our lives?

In Matthew 4, after Jesus was baptized by John, He was led into the wilderness by the Spirit of God to be tested by the Devil. After fasting for forty days and forty nights, the Devil appeared to Him and tempted Him in three ways: personal desire (turning stones into bread), ego and pride (proving He was the Messiah), and power (bowing down to Satan to receive power). Jesus overcame each one of these temptations and afterward launched His ministry. We know His ministry was incredibly effective, powerful, and Spirit-led.

It is no different with us.

You will be tempted in three areas: personal desire, ego and pride, and power. You will be called to do it a different way. You will struggle with heart issues of jealousy, pride, anger, and the like. You will question why people seem to have it easier than you, and you'll fight pride when you're through the hard part. You'll want to defend yourself because as time passes, it seems your credibility is the only thing moving but not in a good direction.

There will be a temptation to turn stones into bread because you're hungry for the next thing God has for you. It will feel like it's been forty days since you've been commissioned by God and after not having food, you're hungry to do what He has called you to do.

We turn stones into bread by seeking the approval of people instead of resting in God's approval of us. We turn stones into bread by putting ourselves into positions God has not yet appointed us to be in. It's like we're worried He won't follow through with what He said He would do.

There will be a temptation to rest for a while and not the rest that's good for us. It's the rest where the enemy wants us. The rest where we decide to coast and quit pursuing what God has for us. You'll hear the lie that it's easier to conform to what is happening instead of continuing to stand in faith.

If you've been in a situation with people who aren't changing, even though you feel called by God to impact their lives, you'll be faced with the temptation to treat them the way they've treated you. You'll hear the lie that it's not a big deal, you're a Christian, you can hear God, so you're in a safe place in judging them.

All of these are rooted in the belief that God isn't going to do as He said, so we need to get comfortable and prepare for the long haul.

How you pioneer will largely determine *what* you pioneer. If you're pioneering from the flesh, you'll pioneer what's *of* the flesh.

> *Do not be deceived: God cannot be mocked. A man reaps what he sows. Whoever sows to please their flesh, from the flesh will reap destruction; whoever sows to please the Spirit, from the Spirit will reap eternal life.* (Galatians 6:7-8 NIV)

There is no denying you have something unique and special within you. You're a carrier of His glory, so I would expect nothing less. I wrote this book because I believe we are in an incredible time. We have intelligent people surrounding us starting business endeavors, creating new ideas and inventions, speaking more boldly, and stepping away from the status quo. Unless we harness our selfish desire of "doing it ourselves," and surrender it to God, we're going to have a lot of "Towers of Babel" that end up being destroyed because we're not meant to carry the power of selfish desires.

Satan is the father of lies and the father of pride. He was cast out of heaven along with one third of the angels in heaven as a result of this pride. Scripture repeats that pride ends in downfall. We can try to raise ourselves up to a level of power, but we cannot sustain it. We will tumble and tumble hard.

When we walk in humility and surrender to God, what is built is a platform for God's glory to shine throughout the Earth.

You're reading this because you wanted to know how to do it a different way. You wanted to know how to thrive in doing the new thing, and you wanted answers to help you step into your God-given destiny. My prayer is you take this book to heart and to the throne room of Heaven, asking if there's any area He would like you to work on. My prayer is you understand the magnitude of what He's called you to do, and you know He isn't going anywhere. We cannot do anything in our own power, but by His strength, power, and love, we can withstand the pressures of temptation and give Him the glory.

I want to end with this scripture:

*Let us not become weary in doing good, for at the proper time
we will reap a harvest if we do not give up.*
(Galatians 6:9, NIV)

Much love to you, my friend. Don't lose heart.

NOTES

1. Groeschel, Craig. 2019. "If it's God's time you can't force it. When it is God's time you can't stop it!" August 1, 2019. https://www.facebook.com/life.church/ posts/10157229922938796?comment_ id=10157286152153796&comment_tracking=%7B%22t-n%22%3A%22R%22%7D.

2. "Haven't Seen It Yet." #3 on Haven't Seen It Yet. Sparrow, 2019, Digital download. Danny Gokey, Colby Wedgeworth, & Ethan Hulse. 2019.

3. Savelle Foy, Terri. "Warm Up Time! 5 Exercises to Stretch Your Thinking and Prepare You for Your Dreams." Terri Savelle Foy Ministries. https://www.terri.com/warm-up-time-5-exercises-to-stretch-your-thinking-and-prepare-you-for-your-dreams/ (accessed January 1, 2019).

4. Wooden, John. n.d. "A Quote by John Wooden." Goodreads. Goodreads. Accessed July 20, 2020. https://www. goodreads.com/quotes/8337239-when-opportunity-comes-it-s-too-late-to-prepare.

5. Online Parallel Bible Project. "Strong's Greek: 659.

Ἀποτίθημι (Apotithémi) — to Put off, Lay Aside." Bible Hub. https://biblehub.com/greek/659.htm (accessed July 14, 2020).

6. Merriam-Webster, s.v. "surrender," accessed July 20, 2020, https://www.merriam-webster.com/dictionary/surrender.

7. Alton Eugene, "History," YouTube video, 11:02, April 23, 2018, https://www.youtube.com/watch?v=IRj982d1EWw.

8. Called to Flag LTD. "Color Reference for Worship Flags." Called to Flag. https://www.calledtoflag.com/color-meanings.

9. Online Parallel Bible Project. "Strong's Greek: 3306. Μένω (Menó) — to Stay, Abide, Remain." Bible Hub. https://biblehub.com/greek/3306.htm (accessed April 17, 2020).

10. Ruckert Abendmahl. Online Parallel Bible Project. Bible Hub. July 23, 2020. https://biblehub.com/greek/3306.htm.

11. Watts, Jon. Spiderman: Homecoming. 2017; Hollywood; Sony Picture Motion Picture Group; June 28, 2017.

12. Forbes. "How To Train Like An Olympian." 2008. Forbes, July 8, 2008. https://www.forbes.com/2008/07/08/training-perfect-athlete-olympics08-forbeslife-cx_avd_0708health.html.

13. Augustyn, Adam. "Tower of Babel | Mythological Tower, Babylonia." In Encyclopedia Britannica. The Editors of Encyclopedia Britannica, 2019. https://www.britannica.com/topic/Tower-of-Babel.

ACKNOWLEDGMENTS

I've always heard authors say they could write a book thanking everyone who supported them in the process of writing but never understood it until I was in the midst of it myself. While I'd love to go through and mention people by name, I simply can't. But there are a few I want to call out.

My husband: I don't need to say much more than you embody the role of the Ephesians 5 husband well. You've sacrificed so much for me to be able to walk in what God has called me to do. I am so thankful for your encouragement, prayers, and support. I wouldn't be doing this without you.

My family: Y'all have watched me hit the ground running, run into walls, fail, and try again. Not once have you discouraged me from walking out what God has called me to do--even if I look a little crazy. Thank you for your support.

Liz Hughes: Sis, THANK YOU. That's all I can say. From day one of writing this book to helping me launch it, you've been an incredible supporter and friend. Your help and support as my launch assistant helped me not to lose my mind in the final stages.

United House Publishing: I have prayed for a publishing company that would be iron for me, support, sharpens, and joins their vision with mine. From teaming up as an author and joining the team as a coach, you've truly become family, and I am so thankful for every one of you.

For everyone who has played a part in this, even through prayer or encouragement, THANK YOU. You have held me up when I couldn't hold myself up. You've spoken into and over me at the time I needed it the most. You are so dear to me, and I thank God for you daily.

I thank God daily for His call on my life, equipping me to fulfill it, and His grace to endure the hard places.

ABOUT THE AUTHOR

Taylor Phillips is a Jesus lover, wife, stay-at-home dog mom, and writer. She is wildly passionate about helping people restructure their life, discover who they are in Christ, and living in the fullness of that identity with boldness and excellence. When she's not writing, she pretends she's a gourmet chef by living vicariously through competitors on Chopped. *Training Ground: From Anointing to Appointing* is her debut book.

Social media:
Instagram: @tayn_phillips
Facebook: Taylor Phillips - Author

CPSIA information can be obtained
at www.ICGtesting.com
Printed in the USA
LVHW052013110121
676217LV00023B/1037/J